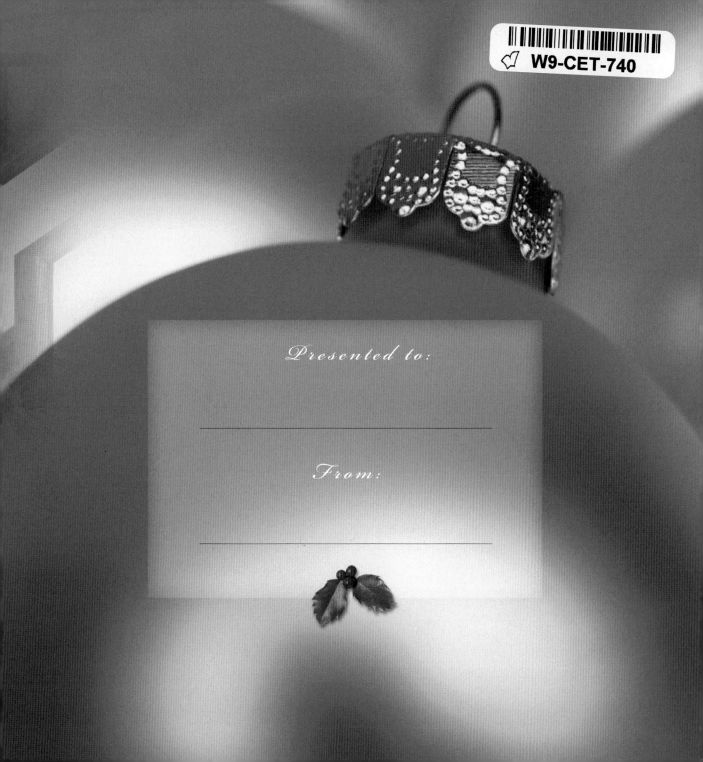

Presented to:

_____

From:

_____

Project Editor: Pat Matuszak

Designed by Uttley/DouPonce DesignWorks,
Sisters, Oregon

Recipes by Vestal Goodman are taken from *Cooking with Vestal and Friends,*
Copyright©1999 by Happy House. All rights reserved. Used by permission.

Gaither Event Photography: Russ Harrington

ISBN 0-8499-9566-3

Printed and bound in Belgium

BILL & GLORIA
GAITHER
P R E S E N T

A

Christmas

HOMECOMING

Our Favorite Christmas Memories, Songs, and Recipes

J. COUNTRYMAN

NASHVILLE, TENNESSEE

A Christmas Homecoming

Anyone can look around at us—this patchwork quilt bunch of Homecoming friends—and see that we are all very different: different ages, different backgrounds, different musical styles, even different hairstyles (no offense, Bill). But the common thread woven through our relationships is our love for each other, our family, our tradition, our singing, and our sweet, sweet Savior. Christmas seems to celebrate, better than any other time, all the things that mean the most to us. And we invite you, as an extension of the Homecoming family, to join the festivities!

So many of us come from a southern heritage where it is understood that our holiday will include a home-cooked Christmas dinner, extended family gatherings, and deep roots of yearly tradition and of faith. The same familiar carols each and every year immerse our spirits in the realization that this perfect Being came to our imperfect world. He is our song; His life—our cause to love one other! The birth of Christ was the first breath of our eternity—the fundamental core of our belief.

We want to share ourselves with you as we share our favorite Christmas stories, traditions, and joys in this little book. Consider it another package under the tree—our gift to you—as a token of appreciation for the love and warmth we feel from city to city, throughout the year, throughout the world.

Joy and peace this miraculous season,

GLORIA GAITHER

Ready, Set, Christmas!

For the Gaither family, Christmas starts on Thanksgiving afternoon as soon as the dinner is over and the dishes cleared. Young and old alike gather around the craft table to make the 'decorations' for the first Christmas tree of the season: a tree for the wildlife. This is how we remind ourselves and teach the children that Christmas is about 'the least of these.' It is a time to give blessing and supply needs in the name of Jesus.

Together we string popcorn; put floral wires through cranberries to make cranberry circles; tie peanuts in the shell by their 'waists' with colorful yarn to make peanut garlands; spread pinecones with peanut butter then roll them in birdseed; and make other things that will attract and feed birds, squirrels, rabbits and opossums.

Then we take these decorations and hang them on a live pine tree in our yard. The children hang things on the lower branches; the taller 'kids' trim the higher branches. Then, until Christmas, we watch the tree making 'provision for the small creatures.'*

On the Sunday after Thanksgiving, a real Christmas tree goes up in the living room and the whole house begins a joyful renovation from its regular apparel to the glittering dress of Christmas. Parties (like 'Soup and Carols') and baking nights, sledding and snowman building, wrapping packages and welcoming visitors go on until Christmas.

— GLORIA GAITHER

* Instructions for the activity may be found in *Let's Make a Memory* by Gloria Gaither and Shirley Dobson from Word Publishing.

A Date to Celebrate

My favorite Christmas was the one when I got Gloria as my present! Gloria and I got married three days before Christmas, so that year was a total time of rejoicing for us. We just had a wonderful Christmas! We got caught up in celebrating being together as a young newly-wed couple along with the festivities of the holiday. All our usual activities seemed like brand new experiences to me when I looked at them from my new status as a 'husband'—and realized I was now a man with a 'wife.' All our married friends and relatives seemed to regard us differently. They treated us like new members who'd just been initiated into their private club!

We didn't go away for our honeymoon. We spent our first night in Fort Wayne, then the next night and morning at our parents' homes celebrating Christmas. It was more important to us to be with our families than to visit some exotic place for our first week of marriage.

—BILL GAITHER

As Old As Bill

I'm getting ready to enjoy all those big Christmas dinners. I eat anything I want. I like Christmas so much that I plan to be around for a thousand more Christmases! Part of my plan is that I don't eat any of that health food junk. I need all the preservatives I can get if I'm going to be just as well-preserved as Bill Gaither when I get to be a thousand years old!

—MARK LOWRY

The Right Number

The Christmas memory that stands out in my mind began with an urgent message from a stranger. My wife, LaBreeska, and I came home from shopping and found that a lady we didn't know had called our house. She sounded quite upset in the message she'd left on our answering machine—she obviously didn't know she'd reached the wrong number. She thought she'd dialed an organization in our town that provides food for needy families at Christmas time. She gave her name and address and then said that someone else had gotten the food basket the volunteers had left for her family. Well, my wife and I looked at each other and said, 'She's got the wrong number.' Then we realized that the organization would never know about the lady's problem and we wanted to do something to help. She hadn't left a phone number I could call to tell her the message hadn't reached the people she'd intended. So I went out and bought a ham and a big box of food. Then I drove around downtown in the projects, searching until I found the address she'd given. I went upstairs and knocked on the door. That family was so excited to see someone had come out to help them. They were truly thankful for all the food. I placed it on their table, wished them all a merry Christmas, and went on my way. As I was going down the stairs, tears came to my eyes. I prayed, 'Oh Lord, when people call in need, please don't ever let my number be the wrong number.'

—JOEL HEMPHILL

A Christmas Eve Visitor

I couldn't have been much more than four or five years old, so the events of my most memorable Christmas Eve may be a little different than I remember them. What I remember was that our family was in the living room of the upstairs apartment where we lived. We were watching one of those claymation Christmas Eve specials you usually find on TV during this time of year.

All of a sudden, Mom snatched up my brother and me and made for the hallway bathroom as fast as she could with two preschoolers in her arms. She carried us away like we were being kidnapped, dashing into the tiny room and locking the door. She held us close and told us to be as quiet as possible so the person coming down the hallway wouldn't hear us and know we were in there.

That was when we heard him. His steps were heavy and deliberate. Soon they stopped in front of the bathroom door. Mom asked us to peek under and see who it was. We saw a pair of shiny black boots and, as he continued down the hall, we could hear the sound of jingle bells. He was telling someone to be very quiet so they wouldn't wake the two good little boys who lived in the house. It didn't seem odd to a four-year-old that Santa was talking very loudly and doing a lot of loud ho-hoing.

My brother, Mark, and I stared at each other. We couldn't believe it. Santa was actually in our house, and we were fooling him by hiding in the bathroom. He took the bag he dragged down the hall into the living room where the Christmas tree was waiting to be filled. It was all we could do to keep from screaming with delight as he'd read the tag on each gift: 'Here's one for little Kenny. He's been such a good boy this year. . . .And here's one for Mark. What did you say? No, I don't believe he's been too ornery to get a gift.'

We never did wonder where Dad was hiding while all of this was going on. We never thought to ask him. He missed it though, and my brother and I were all too happy to tell him about it when we finally got out of the bathroom.

—KENNY BISHOP

RECIPE FOR KENNY BISHOP'S CHRISTMAS WASSAIL

5 quarts of apple cider
1-1/4 cup brown sugar
6 ounces frozen lemon juice concentrate
6 ounces frozen orange juice concentrate
7-1/2 whole cloves and allspice
1-1/4 tablespoons ground nutmeg
30 cinnamon sticks

Put cider, sugar and fruit juices in a large pot. Tie cloves and allspice in a cheesecloth. Add to cider with nutmeg. Cover and simmer for 30 minutes. Remove spice bag. Serve hot with a cinnamon stick in each mug.

What a Surprise!

My sister Faye was always afraid of anything furry—especially mice! One Christmas my son Rick folded up a furry stuffed mouse into a little bitty box and gave it to Faye. She thought such a tiny package couldn't possibly have anything in it that could scare her, but when she took the lid off, the mouse had been folded up so tightly that it 'jumped' out. She screamed out loud! After that whenever she got a box that had a tag that read 'To Aunt Faye, From Rick,' she always had someone else open it for her.

One Christmas dessert that will surprise your family in a good way is Double Chocolate Fantasy Bars. Its great chocolate flavor will 'jump' out when you take a bite.

—VESTAL GOODMAN

RECIPE FOR VESTAL'S DOUBLE CHOCOLATE FANTASY BARS

1 package chocolate cake mix
1/3 cup of oil
1 egg
1 cup chopped nuts
1 can sweetened condensed milk

1 package semi-sweet chocolate chips
1 teaspoon vanilla extract
dash of salt

DIRECTIONS:

In a large mixing bowl, beat cake mix, oil and egg on medium speed until crumbly. Add nuts. Reserve 1-1/2 cups of crumb mixture, and press the remainder firmly on bottom of greased 13 by 9-inch pan. In small saucepan, combine remaining ingredients. Over medium heat, cook and stir until chips melt. Pour evenly over prepared crust. Top with reserved crumb mixture. Bake 25 to 30 minutes in a 350-degree oven or until bubbly. Cool and cut into bars. Store loosely covered at room temperature.

My Daddy's Home!

I grew up in Indiana. My dad worked for a local company that seemed to always lay off their employees around the holidays. Lay-offs were financially hard on my family since we were already struggling to make ends meet. One year, when I was around seven or eight, my dad decided to move to Queens, New York in November and work for a couple of months to be able to provide a stable income and to guarantee us a good Christmas. After two weeks, he got to missing us so badly that he moved us up to New York with him. We were scared in this new big city. We knew no one. The different language and culture were too much for us. We moved back to Indiana after only a couple of weeks. We realized when we left my dad in Queens that we probably wouldn't see him until late January. That meant he wouldn't be home for Christmas.

On Christmas Eve that year, guess who showed up unexpectedly? Yep, Dad flew in just to be with us. He was home only twelve hours before he had to fly back. I have no idea what gifts I got; all I remember is that Dad was home. My brother and I ran up to him and cried, 'You're home! Daddy's home!'

— ERNIE HAASE

16

Cherished Memories

At Christmas we always remember loved ones who have gone to be with Jesus. These past sixty years my brother and I have met at our folks' house for Christmas Eve. On his last Christmas on earth, Danny put forth a great effort to get there. During the course of painful treatment for cancer, he kept saying how he thought things were looking up. Danny took any tough circumstance and put the best face on it. I'll cherish that memory for a long time.

—BILL GAITHER

My Favorite Christmas Recipe

My favorite Christmas recipe is a concoction called Cheese Date Goodies. Kathy fixes these wonderful morsels every Christmas and they are something to look forward to.

I need to say a few words about Kathy's prowess in the kitchen. Whereas God gave me a talent to sing and write the occasional song, He didn't give me any abilities in the food department. I'm one of those burn-water guys. If it's my night to cook, the kids all pile into the car and ask where we're going. Get the picture?

Kathy, on the other hand, is a wizard in the kitchen and is known far and wide for the talent and artistry she brings to food. Don't take my word for it. Ask any of the Homecoming friends who sing on the recording sessions in Nashville. They will all turn into poets singing Kathy's praises. I wonder at times if the only reason I'm invited to work on these sessions is because there may be a chance of one or more of Kathy's culinary delights making it to the gig. As a matter of fact, some of the guys have even said so to my face. That's okay by me. She's that good and it makes me proud of her abilities.

— STEPHEN HILL

RECIPE FOR KATHY HILL'S CHEESE DATE GOODIES

PASTRY:

1 stick butter

1 teaspoon salt

2 cups sharp cheddar cheese

A dash of red pepper to taste

1-1/2 cups plain flour

FILLING:

1 8-ounce package chopped dates

1/4 cup water

1/2 cup light brown sugar

1/2 cup chopped walnuts

DIRECTIONS:

Grate cheese and mix other pastry ingredients until dough can be rolled. Cut with small biscuit cutter. Cut dates into pieces, and mix with other filling ingredients and cook until thick and fairly dry. Cool. Add nuts. Put small amount of filling on half the cheese biscuit. Fold over other side and mash edges together. Bake at 325 degrees for 15 to 20 minutes. Yields 2 to 3 dozen.

*I use a food processor for the pastry. Just throw everything in and mix until the dough forms a ball. Yum, yum—enjoy!

Christmas Pajamas

We were asked to be a part of some Christmas video footage to be shot at the home of Anthony and Eva Burger. We had to shoot it in July in order for it to be ready in time for Christmas. So, on the scheduled night, I loaded up all my crew with all our winter clothes and headed to Anthony's for the session. As you can imagine, it was really hot in Nashville in July, so getting the kids to wear fleeces and winter attire was quite the challenge. The house was all decorated for Christmas, complete with snow and everything. The director had chosen the scene and everyone was in costume except for me. I thought I'd wear some jeans and a shirt like I might around our house. But no. My wife thought I should be in my pajamas like everyone else. Well, this might have been normal, except that the pajamas she packed for me to be seen in by the entire TV audience were my bright red, drop-drawer long johns. But, after some very understandable resistance from me, she won. Consequently, I believe I am the first of the Homecoming artists to appear in one of our videos in his 'long handles.'

— GUY PENROD

That Holiday Feeling

I am actually thankful for the malls at Christmas. Even though they seem to be encouraging commercialization of the holiday, I have seen something deeper going on there. I find it exciting to watch the crowds of people going out of their way to find just the right gifts to express their love for others. Only at this time of year do hearts open so wide to love. Suddenly this huge secular marketplace outside the church recruits carolers to sing the story of the birth of the Savior for everyone to hear. The secular and the spiritual parts of our lives come together in a beautiful, harmonic experience.

—BILL GAITHER

The Nod

Every Christmas, for as long as I can remember, we have traveled to the North Carolina mountains to my Grandma's house. The Haas Family usually gets together on the Saturday before Christmas. There is always more food and goodies than you can imagine. About forty-five of us children, grandchildren, and great-grandchildren can't wait to get to the presents, the daddies can't wait for the food, and Grandma just can't wait for the singin' to start.

My Grandma Haas was the choir director at her church for fifty years. She loved teaching people how to sing 'the right way, by shaped notes, of course.' Christmas is no different. After we eat, we all gather together, Mom on the piano; Dad, Uncle O.C., and Uncle Rex on the guitars. Sounds like a song already. Grandma, 'Miss Edith' is what her choir called her, passes out the old green caroling books—the ones with all our babies' teeth marks on them. We always start out with page one and work our way toward the end of the songbook, until the little kids get so rowdy that they are louder than our singing. If you look around the room there are always a couple of quartets and trios forming and waiting for the nod—we all know 'the nod.' That's when it is your time to sing out and make Grandma smile. Uncle Larry always shouts a little when all the harmonies fill in and we hit another chorus of "O Beautiful Star of Bethlehem."

Today when I get on the stage at many Gaither concerts, I think of my Grandma and how she and my family helped me learn to sing. It's funny how, after all these years, I'm still sitting 'round a piano singing, except now it is with a few thousand friends! But we all still wait and look for 'the nod'—the only difference is that it comes from Bill Gaither.

—WESLEY PRITCHARD

O come all ye faithful,

Joyful and triumphant!

She's Home!

We always looked forward to spending Christmas at my parents' home. There was a big porch that went all the way across the front of the old farmhouse filled with rocking chairs and swings. As I turned in the drive, I'd see my favorite uncle, Ernest, and my daddy waiting there for me. When I would come down the road, they would start jumping up and down and hollering, 'Okay, the party can start now. She's here!' We had such a wonderful time. We all stayed in that house together with all the children and cousins and grandchildren. We slept on quilts on the floor and on couches all over the house. It was heavenly. One of my favorite treats to make and share with family was rich and hearty Molasses Cookies.

—VESTAL GOODMAN

RECIPE FOR VESTAL GOODMAN'S MOLASSES COOKIES

1/2 cup shortening	1 teaspoon salt
3/4 cup sugar	2 teaspoons ginger
1 egg	1 teaspoon cinnamon
1-1/4 cups molasses	1 teaspoon nutmeg
4-1/2 cups flour	1 teaspoon cloves
2 teaspoons soda	1 cup boiling water

FROSTING

2 cups confectioner's sugar	1 teaspoon lemon extract
1 tablespoon butter	3 tablespoons milk

DIRECTIONS:

Combine shortening, sugar, egg and molasses. Mix well. Sift together flour, soda, salt, ginger, cinnamon, nutmeg and cloves. Stir into molasses mixture. Add water, stirring until smooth. Drop by teaspoonfuls onto lightly greased cookie sheet. Bake for 8 to 10 minutes at 400 degrees. After cookies are cooled, ice with frosting below.

More Than a Story

If I live to be a hundred, I will never forget the feeling on Christmas mornings when my sister would summon me from a deep sleep and whisper, 'Let's go see if Santa Claus has come!' We'd stand together in the doorway of the dark kitchen, poised, hands on the light switch, anticipating the surprises, hoping he'd found his way to our house again. It never seemed quite reasonable for him to come bearing gifts for two little girls who didn't even know him. We couldn't explain it. We just knew he came.

All these years later, I've learned to smile at the irony of the ageless legend whom we so innocently perceived as the bearer of Christmas. I embrace the reality of the One who came so far just to assure there would ever be a Christmas at all. Christ came to us before we knew He existed. He paid the ultimate sacrifice because He longed for us to know Him. When we were indifferent to His voice, He kept calling. When we turned away, He kept reaching. He made Himself lowly just to walk among us. He was not concerned with our wit or talent or comeliness. He never chose to explain His love or to reason it out. It just was.

We were indifferent to His sacrifice. We didn't invite Him or woo Him or love Him back. But He came. Thank God He came! It is beyond our realm of possibility to understand the way He loves us. It is unreasonable. It is illogical. He just does. He just can't help it.

One thing more: Should you manage even a slight pause from the bustling demands of the holidays, pour a cup of hot chocolate, turn down the lights, sit back and savor this wonderful season He has brought to you once again. Consider His faithfulness in days past and His careful planning of days to come. Anticipate the surprises. Then throw on the light switch and CELEBRATE! It's Christmas!

—JANET PASCHAL

The Christmas Proposal

Our favorite Christmas memory was in 1984. Jeff and I had been dating for a few months, and he had discussed getting me a piece of jewelry for Christmas. I suspected it was an engagement ring, but I wasn't certain.

When he returned from the jewelry store, I asked if he had my present, and he told me to get it out of the glove compartment. As I opened the glove compartment, he had cued up the song "The Greatest Gift Of All," so that the song was playing as I opened the Christmas gift he had bought for me—a beautiful engagement ring.

—JEFF & SHERI EASTER

RECIPE FOR _____ SHERI EASTER'S SAUSAGE ROLL

1 pound of sausage
2 cups self-rising flour
8 ounces cream cheese
1 stick of butter

On Christmas Eve I prepare a sausage roll, so on Christmas morning we can have a good breakfast with a minimum of work.

DIRECTIONS:
Mix flour, cream cheese and butter together to make dough. Sprinkle sausage onto dough and roll up. Refrigerate, then slice and bake at 450 degrees for 12 to 15 minutes.

Two Very Different Christmas Services

A few friends and I had been asked to conduct a service in the chapel of the state penitentiary in Nashville. It was my first time at a maximum-security facility and this place was scary—'the Big House' in every sense.

We passed through very tight security, and then we set up our equipment in the chapel area. Just a few inmates trickled in. Out of a huge prison population only 25 or 30 men showed up for the service. The whole affair seemed very awkward at the outset as we began to sing Christmas carols rather uneasily and self-consciously. However, I soon began to notice some of the men closing their eyes in worship. It occurred to me to ask whether anyone would like to stand up and offer a testimony.

One man stood and declared, 'I praise God that I'm here tonight, because it took coming to this place for me to discover His love and mercy for me.' A few inmates agreed saying 'Amen' as he sat down. Another inmate stood and smiled: 'I just want to say that I'm freer inside these walls than I ever was on the outside.' A few 'hallelujahs' joined the 'amens'. One after another, men stood to give praise to the One who calls us out of darkness into His marvelous light. What a church service we were having!

Finally a brother stood up and declared, 'This is all the world needs, what we've got here tonight. If a bunch of criminals can come together and experience the forgiveness of God and know the fellowship of His Holy Spirit and feel this much love, then that's all anybody else needs.'

You should have heard the 'hallelujahs'— mine was as loud as anybody's.

The next night I was performing at a fundraising event. The people who attended were well-dressed and affluent. It was a beautiful night of music, celebration, and fun. Toward the end I spoke about the real meaning of Christmas: that Jesus came as a poor, humble servant to take our place on the cross to pay for our sins. Quite a few people seemed uncomfortable, self-conscious and unsure of how to respond as the message of the cross intruded upon the gaiety of our evening.

It occurred to me that though everyone there would probably have claimed to be a Christian, somehow we were missing out on something that had become true treasure for those inmates the night before. Those humble prisoners deeply realized that Christ was all they needed. Though outwardly prisoners, they were free to really know and experience the One who had come to set captives free.

—BUDDY GREENE

My Favorite Present

It's hard to choose one gift of all the wonderful presents people have given me as my favorite Christmas present. But my husband, Howard, knows how much I love jewelry. Right after I was healed of heart disease, he bought me my big diamond cluster ring in Bethlehem while we were there on a Holy Land trip. He said, 'That looks like you.'

The best present is to have my kids and my grandkids home for Christmas—that's all it takes to make my holiday a success. I get to cook for them and to tell those precious children the Christmas story. We celebrate the birth of our Savior together. It's an exciting, real story! Children deserve to know it today.

—VESTAL GOODMAN

RECIPE FOR **VESTAL'S CHRISTMAS CHOCOLATE PIE**

3 eggs, lightly beaten

1 cup white Karo syrup

1/2 cup white sugar

1/2 cup chocolate chips

2 tablespoons butter, melted

1 teaspoon vanilla

1-1/2 cups pecans

9-inch unbaked pie shell

DIRECTIONS:

Mix all ingredients in a large bowl. Pour into a 9-inch unbaked pie shell. Bake in 350-degree oven for 50 to 60 minutes or until a knife inserted in the filling will come out clean.

Home for Christmas

A Christmas memory that stands out in my mind happened when I was four years old. Every night when I was little, we used to say our bedtime prayers and we always remembered to pray for my older brother who was in the army. We all looked up to him and missed him so much. We did the same on Christmas Eve, 1944. Then six siblings nestled down in their beds, asleep (at least I was) in our farmhouse in rural North Carolina. Suddenly loud talking from the living room disturbed the quiet night. It awakened us and we got up yawning and rubbing our eyes to go and see what was happening. We peeped around the corner and saw a sight that made us crow with delight! Standing by the Christmas tree, handsomely dressed in his army uniform, our beloved older brother smiled down at us. He had come home on a short Christmas pass before shipping out for Germany. We all ran for him with hugs and cheers! It was pandemonium for a while. Then we noticed our Christmas stockings hanging from the mantle. They were all filled except one. We concluded that our brother had scared off Santa because he didn't get to finish his job. But we didn't really care. I'll never forget the look on my mom and dad's faces—their son was home.

—CONNIE HOPPER

A Little Cowboy

My mom spent endless hours baking and cooking in preparation for Christmas with her eleven children. When we were little, the baked Christmas delicacies were plentiful but toys seemed non-existent at our house. One Christmas memory that's outstanding was when my dad bought me a Gene Autry holster set. That's the only toy I remember getting as a boy and I cherish the memory.

— CLAUDE HOPPER

Christmas Cookies

The first time Rex invited me to his hometown, Asheville, North Carolina, to meet his mother and family was at Christmas. We were both shy and quiet as we drove up the mountain to the place where he had been born and lived until he had left to join his first full-time quartet (The Homeland Harmony) in Atlanta. As we traveled up the winding road, I was surprised that he began to honk his horn to let the neighbors know he was back home. Later in the day he drove me through the neighborhood with his mother, Marietta Nelon, his sister Judy, and his Aunt Faye. Suddenly Rex pulled the car over in front of a house and bolted up to the door alone. He went into this house without even knocking. Rex's Mother smiled: 'We probably won't be here long. Rex has just gone in to get his tin of his favorite cookies that Mrs. Knighten has baked for him all of his life.' And, sure enough, in just a matter of minutes he was back in the car with a tin of cookies under his arm. He reluctantly opened the top and offered me one, warning, 'And I mean just one. These are mine!' I learned that day that those cookies were his favorite thing in the world to eat. Later I asked Mildred Knighten if she would mind sharing this special recipe with me. She did. And now I would like to share this with you. Along with his mother's cooking, it was something he looked forward to experiencing again each Christmas in Asheville.

—JUDY NELON

RECIPE FOR _____ REX NELON'S DATE NUT COOKIES

1 package of dates (about 40)
1 cup of sugar
1-1/2 cups of flour
1/2 teaspoon baking soda
1/2 teaspoon salt
1 cup of brown sugar

1-1/2 cup of rolled oats
(uncooked)
1/2 pound of melted butter
1/2 cup chopped nuts (pecans)

DIRECTIONS:
Cut dates into pieces, cook with water and sugar until thick.
Set aside to cool. Mix dry ingredients, oats, and melted
butter, then mix until crumbly. Add nuts. Layer crumbs in a
13 by 9-inch pan, reserving 1/3 of mixture for topping.
(Mildred's husband, Gordon, says the secret is that their pan
is fifty years old.) Finish top with remaining mixture. Bake
at 325 degrees for 30 to 35 minutes. Cut into squares. They
are so good! Can be frozen to await special visitors!

My Favorite Student

I cherish so many wonderful memories of Christmas; but one Christmas stands out above the others as my favorite memory. That year I was just a little girl, and I found the doll of my dreams waiting for me under the tree. Of all the dolls I ever had, 'Suzy Smart' was my favorite. I have always loved everything about school. I loved the classroom and the smell of fresh chalk on the board. I loved construction paper and glue. And of course, the times when there was music in the classroom. I can still see the upright piano sitting in the corner of my first-grade classroom. Every once in a while, Mrs. Melvin, my first grade teacher, would allow me to sit at the piano to sing and play for my classmates. That made an indelible impression on me and I knew from that moment on that I wanted to be a teacher. So, on Christmas morning when I saw Suzy Smart sitting there under the Christmas tree, I was simply delighted. Like the perfect student waiting for class to begin, she sat behind her student desk wearing a plaid uniform and patent leather shoes. She also came with a chalkboard complete with chalk and an eraser. When I would pull the string that made her talk, she would spell, add, and sing. Suzy Smart became my favorite student and, of course, I was her favorite teacher.

Years have gone by since Suzy Smart and I played school together in our imaginary classroom. But my love for learning and seeing students enjoy the learning process continues.

Before going into the music ministry full time, I felt blessed to teach middle school music and English for several years. And now I'm back in the classroom teaching songwriting to college students. Isn't that just like God to use something that was once considered child's play to make a life-long impression on the heart?

—BABBIE MASON

White Christmas

If I ever sing a Christmas song at a concert, I sing "I'm Dreaming of a White Christmas" because that song just feels good. In the Nashville area we don't always get snow at Christmas, but we still dream of it, anyway!

—VESTAL GOODMAN

Christmas Eve at the Gaithers'

On Christmas Eve the Gaither side of the family goes to Bill's parents' house for a noisy gathering with lots of food and children. On Christmas morning, I bake our traditional dish of homemade biscuits and delicious chipped beef gravy. This is the only time this specialty is prepared all year. Our children and their children, and anyone else who is around, come to breakfast at the big oak table.

Afterward we gather around the tree for worship and the Christmas story. When the kids were at home, they all slept in sleeping bags around the Christmas tree on Christmas Eve, but now they have Christmas with their own families, then come for breakfast and the opening of gifts.

On Christmas afternoon we all get together with my sister, Evelyn, her husband, Dave, and our children's families. We have a nutritious dinner, open presents and play games until we're all too sleepy to stay any longer.

—GLORIA GAITHER

At the Phelps' Home

A typical Christmas at our home involves the entire family gathering together in one place, either at our house or at the home of my parents or one of my sisters. We stay together as long as we can and do lots of cooking (Mom's chicken-fried steak and tea cakes are required staples), watch lots of movies and spend lots of time playing with the kids—snow and fireplaces are not optional. On Christmas Eve, we attend church candlelight services if we can. Before any presents are exchanged, we always read the Christmas story together—nobody does it better than my dad. On Christmas morning, the kids are up early to discover Santa's gifts—fireside 'tracks' on the hearth and half-eaten cookies. It's not Christmas if you can see the rug under all the wrapping paper! After it's all over, we relax and soon venture out to find the nearest movie theater playing a kids' movie or the nearest store to buy more Diet Coke while we try to forget that someone is soon going to have to leave and return home.

I love Zephaniah 3:17; 'The Lord your God is with you, he is mighty to save. He will take great delight in you, he will quiet you with his love, he will rejoice over you with singing' (NIV). This verse speaks of peace, salvation, and God's presence, love, and joy. It presents a beautiful picture of God singing over us—everything that Christmas means. As far as I've been able to determine, this is the only time in the Scripture we find God singing. And He's singing 'over' me, about me rather than to me. I love this.

—DAVID PHELPS

RECIPE FOR _____ DAVID PHELPS' MOM'S TEA CAKES

1 cup butter, softened

2 cups sugar

3 eggs

2 tablespoons buttermilk

5 cups all purpose flour

1 teaspoon baking soda

1 teaspoon vanilla

Additional sugar

DIRECTIONS:

Cream butter; gradually add 2 cups sugar, beating well. Add eggs, one at a time, beating well after each addition. Add buttermilk, and beat well. Combine flour and soda; gradually stir into creamed mixture. Stir in vanilla. Chill dough several hours or over night.

Roll dough to 1/4-inch thickness on a lightly floured surface, then cut into rounds with a large biscuit cutter. Place on cookie sheet. Bake at 400 degrees for 7 to 8 minutes. Run on the treadmill for 21 minutes per cookie consumed!

The Big Christmas Surprise

I grew up in a pastor's home where love was plentiful, but money often wasn't. Basically there was just enough to pay bills and support seven kids. My six older siblings and I never had a 'big' Christmas like a lot of the kids at school. I remember one year in particular that had been very tough. My mom and dad talked to us and prepared us to face a Christmas morning with few presents under the tree. When my older brothers and sisters understood the problem, they decided to work and save their allowances for enough extra money to give the two youngest of us a 'big' Christmas. They secretly took on extra jobs and saved up for weeks. I realize now how much 'heart' was put into that Christmas. And I will thank them forever!

— IVAN PARKER

Turtle Secrets

At Christmas we are especially thankful for the friends and pioneers who have helped us over the years. We didn't get where we are all by ourselves. What I always say is that if you find a turtle on a fence post, he didn't get there by himself—he had some help! The people who helped us get there today are very dear to us. I love 'em!

—BILL GAITHER

A Christmas of Love

At no time was our family love more tangibly expressed than at Christmas time when we all gathered at Grandmama's house for the 'Big Sumner Christmas.' Big is not an overstatement!

We usually had thirty to forty members of our family around the tree when we started opening gifts every Christmas Eve afternoon. I did say afternoon: Our Grandmama wanted the gifts opened carefully. 'One at a time,' she directed, so she could say 'Ooh' and 'Aah' for each one. It always took four or five hours for her to finally have bragged on each individual present.

In 1953 my dad had just been given an appointment to his first pastorate in a small rural community in central Florida. As usual, we just had to go to Grandmama's house for the 'Big Sumner Christmas,' but we left with just enough cash for gas to put in our old '48 Pontiac and without a single gift to give.

By tradition my Uncle Jake was the gathering's official Santa. About an hour or so into the unwrapping frenzy, Jake noticed that no one had been receiving gifts with the usual tag that read: 'From Buddy, Nell, Donnie and Sharon.' He stood up and excused himself and called Daddy aside. Only in my adult years did I become aware of their conversation from that afternoon.

They returned to the living room and our Santa made a proclamation: 'Y'all take a break. Me and Buddy's gotta do something.' They left and, after an hour or so, returned. Christmas resumed with great gusto. Imagine my joy when I heard our Santa read the tag that said, 'To Donnie, From Mom and Dad.' I always said that was the best bat, ball and glove I ever owned because 'Daddy bought it for me.' My sister smiled real big when Santa read, 'To Sharon, From Mom and Dad' on the tag of a new doll. Grandmama smiled and said, 'What a beautiful doll!'

Thank you, Uncle Jake. You're gone, but still loved. I thank God for the love of Mom and Dad and big brothers. It reminds me of the love of my 'elder brother,' Jesus. One Christmas long ago, God called him aside and asked if he had anything to give. He replied, 'Only my love and my life.' Imagine someone loving us enough to die for us! I'm sure glad I'm in God's family and my wish for this holiday season is that you are, too.

—DONNIE SUMNER

Joy to the World!

The Lord has Come!

Let Earth Receive her King.

More Blessed to Give

When I was growing up, my mom's Ladies' Circle always chose a needy family to bless during the Christmas season. More often than not, my mom would deliver the gifts to the family, and she always took my brothers and me along with her.

We would bring enough food for the family to eat bountifully, clothing for the children and the parents, and each child would get at least one great toy. I will always remember the joy on their faces when they received these gifts. Even as a little girl, it was an emotional event for me; I remember leaving with a grateful heart for the abundance in my life. Mostly, I felt thankful that my family had been able to be a blessing to someone else and that I was able to see how just a little love and caring can make life happier for others.

My mom would always tell the families that Jesus cared about them and wanted to show His love to them at this special season. Afterward, my mom would remind her own children that even though we were not rich in worldly goods, we were blessed by God. It made the presents we got seem so grand and so special. That was proof to me that it is greater to give than to receive.

—SUE DODGE

RECIPE FOR _____ SUE DODGE'S BRUTZEL BARS

1 tube package saltine crackers
1 cup butter (do not use substitutions)
1 cup sugar
1 package (12 ounces) milk chocolate chips
spray-on cooking oil

DIRECTIONS:
Preheat oven to 350 degrees. Line a cookie sheet that has
sides with aluminum foil. Lightly spray with cooking oil.
Arrange saltines in a single layer over the foil. In a medium
sauce-pan, combine butter and sugar and warm to a boil. As
soon as it reaches a bubbling boil, remove from heat and
gently pour over crackers. Bake for 10 minutes or until golden
brown in preheated oven. Remove from oven and rearrange any
crackers that may have moved around. Immediately scatter
chocolate chips over the top. Spread melting chips evenly
with a knife so that they cover the crackers. Cool in
refrigerator for a few hours. Break into pieces before
serving. It tastes like a chocolate toffee bar.

Angels Gather Near

There are many opportunities for outreach during the holiday season. It is our extended family's tradition in all of our homes to adopt a prisoner's child from 'Angel Tree' sponsored by Prison Fellowship. We also have children we support through Compassion International.

Our store, Gaither Family Resources, does a cooperative project each year with a crisis pregnancy center, a shelter for battered women and children, or a center for supplying warm clothing to families in the winter. We love to find tangible ways for children to *give* to other children or to those who are cold, hungry or homeless.

Jesus was born into a family that was far away from home in a strange city with no shelter. They were soon to learn how it felt to be homeless as they fled to Egypt. Jesus often had 'no place to lay His head.' We can in a very real way 'take Him in,' not only into our hearts, but into our homes, kitchens, and arms, because 'whatever we do for the least—we do for Him.'

—GLORIA GAITHER

Christmas Baby?

Our daughter, Sonja, was due to arrive on December twenty-fifth. I was very excited that I might be having a baby on Christmas Day, although that year certainly gave me a new understanding of the Bible's description of Mary as 'great with child'! I was huge with child! As nature would have it, she didn't come that day. I was disappointed, but thought she would surely arrive by New Year's Day. Wrong again! I wondered if she was planning on waiting until the day before she enrolled in kindergarten to be born, but she finally came on January eighth. Though the holidays were pretty uncomfortable, that was a Christmas I'll never forget.

—JEANNE JOHNSON

Thankful Hearts

Christmas of 1991 was very special for me. Earlier that year my dad was involved in a near fatal accident that put him in the hospital for weeks. Then in November of that year, my mother was told she had two large tumors, probably cancerous, and would have to have surgery the week before Christmas. God gave us a wonderful gift that year. He spared my daddy's life, and there was no cancer found in my mom. Needless to say there were many tears of joy from thankful hearts that Christmas.

—CHARLOTTE RITCHIE

Simpler Times

When I was a small boy living on a sharecropper farm in Mississippi, we were very poor. But Christmas was still a special time. Our presents consisted of apples, oranges, and some stick candy. Papa or Mama would read the story of Christ's birth from the Bible and we would have family prayer. Really, these are my fondest memories of Christmas. Today, with so many lavish presents given, I am afraid that the real reason for Christmas has been largely forgotten.

At our little three-room country schoolhouse, we had a big tree decorated with strings of popcorn and different colored paper rings. We decorated it with small candles that we actually lit because there was no electricity for lights like we have today. Our teacher would read the Christmas story from the Bible. What a contrast to today's public schools where no mention of God or the real meaning of Christmas can be made!

—JAMES BLACKWOOD

Power Shopper

About two years before my father passed away, he was quite ill at Christmas. It was a difficult time emotionally for all of us because my dad had always enjoyed Christmas like a big kid. That year he became too weak to enjoy many of our family traditions and spent most of his time lying on the sofa, hoping to participate as much as possible. My oldest daughter, Mallory, was eleven months old and had not started walking yet. She would pull herself up by holding onto furniture and toddle around it. My parents gave her a little shopping cart that was designed to help children learn to walk. We stood her up behind it and she latched onto the handle, leaned forward, and zoomed across the living room under her own power! It was so comical and she had such a surprised look on her face. We all broke into laughter and, of course, she wanted to do it over and over. That was the most I had seen my dad laugh in a long time. It was truly a bright spot in a very dark time in our lives.

—TANYA GOODMAN SYKES

RECIPE FOR TANYA GOODMAN SYKES' CINNAMON ROLLS

3 cups of flour
1/2 teaspoon of salt
1/2 cup of shortening

1 heaping tablespoon of
  baking powder
1 cup of milk

DIRECTIONS:

Mix ingredients together and roll out mixture on a floured board
or waxed paper. Spread with one stick of softened butter or
margarine. Roll in two rolls from each side, from outside
toward the center. Cut down the center to separate the two
rolls. Slice each roll into 1-1/2 inch pieces and stand in a
greased 9 by 13 inch cake pan. Top with syrup (directions below).

SYRUP FOR TOPPING

2 cups of sugar
2 cups of water
2 tablespoons of Karo syrup

DIRECTIONS:

Stir and boil sugar, syrup, and water for one minute.
Then pour mixture over rolls. Don't panic if they
'float'. Bake at 350 degrees for 30 minutes.

A Little Child Shall Lead

At a beautiful auditorium in downtown Birmingham, Alabama, my eyes were dazzled by the crowd of people decked out in reds and greens. The Homecoming friends gathered behind me among the spotlights, cameras and film crew. I was seated on a stool, front and center of the stage, surrounded by Anthony Burger's three darling children and David Phelps' two sweet little girls. As I began singing a song I had co-authored, I was hoping I wouldn't make a mistake doing it this first time on camera. Excitement and adrenaline were running high, and the song was going well. The children were doing a great job of listening and being still throughout the tune. They all were decked out in their finest holiday duds and looked like tiny angels. I could handle all of this until the end of the song. As I got to the last line and started to sing, 'My heart's in the five little fingers of His hand,' I looked down at little Maggie Beth Phelps, about two-and-a-half feet of curly haired perfection, standing as perfectly still as a china doll. She did me in. The tears welled up and my voice cracked. If only I had not chosen that moment to look at little Maggie Beth who was so beautifully framed by the spotlight that she seemed to glow. I was literally overcome by the power of the Lord and His love.

The Bible tells us that '. . . a child shall lead them.' In this instance, a little child brought home the realization of truth to me in a powerful way. Singing about the baby Jesus, surrounded by these sweet children, I was reminded that it truly is for such as these that Christ came.

— STEPHEN HILL

Cutting the Tree

I suppose my favorite Christmas memory would be the first time I can remember going with my dad to the woods on Paris Mountain in South Carolina to find a Christmas tree. How many dads and sons have made the same trek, shivering with fun and cold? I was about five years old and it took lots of little steps to keep up with my dad's big strides. When we found our 'perfect' tree, I could hardly contain my excitement as Dad swung the axe and then offered me a turn! We dragged it through the woods together, feeling quite the manly team. I remember helping Mom and Dad decorate that tree with homemade decorations.

—HOVIE LISTER

Going by the Book?

When I put out a cookbook it was hilarious because I had to go back and actually cook my usual recipes. When I'm cooking you normally won't catch me with a measuring cup and spoon; I just put the stuff in until I feel good about it. But you can't put that into a cookbook. You can't say 'Just put in sugar until you feel good about it.' So we had to make all those recipes and measure as we went so we could write it down for the book.

—VESTAL GOODMAN

RECIPE FOR _____ VESTAL'S COCONUT CAKE

2 cups whipping cream
2 cups sugar
2 cups self-rising flour
4 eggs, separate yolks and whip
  the egg whites

1 teaspoon vanilla
milk from 1 to 2 coconuts

Whip the cream, and then add sugar and flour. Mix egg yolks and vanilla together. Fold in egg whites. Pour into three 9-inch layer cake pans that are lightly greased and floured. Bake at 350 degrees for 45 minutes. After baked, poke holes in cake and pour coconut milk on cake. Allow to cool, then ice with topping below.

FRESH COCONUT ICING

2 unbeaten egg whites
1-1/2 cup of sugar
6 tablespoons of cold water

1/4 teaspoon cream of tartar
1-1/2 teaspoon light corn syrup
1 teaspoon vanilla

Place all ingredients in the top of a double boiler and beat until thoroughly blended. Place over rapidly boiling water in double boiler. Beat 7 minutes. Remove from heat and add 1 teaspoon of vanilla. Ice cake and sprinkle with coconut. (Hint: When I want to save time, I use a cake mix and pour coconut milk over the cake and ice with this recipe.)

A Gift From the Heart

Illness doesn't wait until special celebrations like Thanksgiving and Christmas are over. One year, my mother had been diagnosed with cancer and the surgery had to be scheduled right before the holidays. Her operation went well, and on Christmas morning, mother was with us as the whole family gathered to hear the Nativity story. Our hearts were full of gratitude for having come together through her ordeal. We prayed, thanking God for His amazing gift of eternal life as well as some very special days of being here together.

After all the presents were opened and adored, Bill disappeared into the bedroom. He came back holding some beautifully wrapped boxes. This man who never shops, we were to soon learn, had put a great deal of thought into these small treasures: for Suzanne there was a pair of tiny molded collie dogs in a real Scotch plaid padded bed—collies were very similar to the puppies we had when Suzanne was only five. For Amy he had a pair of delicate little crystal swan, like the pair that swam our creek. For Benjy, now teetering on the front edge of manhood, a velvet box containing a special issue commemorative gold piece. My box revealed a lovely centerpiece of crystal oil-filled candles and two beautiful outfits. Bill gave a special little treasure to mother, as well.

We were all in tears by then, but we all laughed when someone said, 'Dad, now that we know you are capable of all this, we'll expect treasures from you every Christmas . . . and birthday . . . and Easter . . . and Valentine's Day . . . . and . . .'

Mother lived about fifteen years after that, until she was eighty-four, and often reminisced with us about the year Bill made Christmas a gift from the heart.

—GLORIA GAITHER

Christmas in Korea

It was not the best Christmas I can remember, but it's the one that sticks in my mind more than any other: It was 1951. I was a U.S. Marine, sitting on a lonely, cold, and snowy hillside in Korea. It had been snowing for days, and we were on full alert, standing watch all night long. The night was so quiet it seemed like I could hear the snow falling. My favorite Christmas song, "Silent Night," kept running through my mind. I wanted to sing it aloud, but knew that would be too dangerous. However, God gave me such a peace that it seemed to me the angels were caroling in a secret place where only I could hear them. We made it through the night without the attack we were expecting. We all decided that was our Christmas gift from God!

—BOB JOHNSON

Light It Up!

My dad worked the evening shift as a crane operator at Alloy, West Virginia. He and Mother would always set out the presents after he got home from work then wake us up. The way that he woke us up was by setting off firecrackers! When my brothers and I became older teenagers, we decided to play a trick on Dad. When he got in from work at two a.m., we were waiting behind the shrubs with our own firecrackers. You can picture the rest of the story!

—SQUIRE PARSONS

Christmas Puppy

I'm grateful for parents who made sure that Christmas was always special, even during the 'lean' times. One of those times happened when I was six years old. We were living in a rented one-bedroom house in a small rural Kentucky town. My mom and dad had almost no money for Christmas presents, so they went to a barn where there was a new litter of puppies and brought a solid white one home as my present. Naturally, I was thrilled with our Christmas addition. I named him Pal and planned on him becoming my best friend.

On Christmas Eve, dressed in my shepherd-like bathrobe complete with a towel around my head, I slowly walked into our living room and stood by the Christmas tree with Pal in my arms and presented my little lamb-like puppy to Mom and Dad. I think I was trying to give them a gift of what was the most precious to me at the time. What we didn't realize was that this little puppy had been sick since birth and his health was deteriorating. He died before New Years Day. Not a Christmas goes by that I don't think about that little guy and his short, but meaning-ful, contribution to my childhood. I think he was born just to be my gift—to teach me about the Savior who was born to be a gift to the world.

—KEVIN WILLIAMS

Precious Stocking Stuffer

My favorite holiday memory is of Christmas, 1982. Our daughter, Lauren, was born on December eleventh that year. We were living in North Carolina at the time and had planned to go to Tennessee to be with Roger's family for the holidays. We decided to have our own little celebration at home and open our gifts to each other before leaving. We had bought a large stocking with Lauren's name across the top. On the evening we were opening our gifts, we placed our one-week-old daughter in the top of the stocking and took her picture. Then we both sat down on the floor in front of our Christmas tree and placed our baby, all wrapped in her blanket, beside the packages under the tree. Roger would hand me a gift and I would open it, then look at her and cry. I would hand him a gift and he would open it, then look at her and cry. As nice as all the gifts were, nothing could compare to the small bundle lying under our tree.

My favorite recipe is my mom's fresh coconut cake. It's all made from scratch and no one can make it like she can.

— DEBRA TALLEY

RECIPE FOR LAYERED BUTTERMILK COCONUT CAKE

5 eggs

2 cups sugar

3-1/2 cups self-rising flour

3/4 cup Crisco

1-3/4 cup buttermilk

1 teaspoon baking soda

1 teaspoon vanilla

Cream together sugar and Crisco. Mix flour and baking soda. Add to creamed mixture alternately with the buttermilk. Add vanilla. Pour into 4 lightly greased and floured 9-inch cake pans. Bake at 350 degrees. When cake is cool, spread icing (recipe below) between layers, sprinkling coconut on top of each layer of icing, stacking cakes as you go. Finally, ice the whole cake on the outside and sprinkle with coconut.

ICING

3 egg whites

3-1/4 cups sugar

1/4 teaspoon cream of tartar

little less than 1/2 cup water

1 teaspoon vanilla

frozen or fresh coconut

marshmallows

Place egg whites, sugar, cream of tartar, and water in the top of a double boiler. Beat on high speed for 1 minute. Place over boiling water and beat for 6 minutes. Remove from heat and add 1 teaspoon vanilla and beat until it peaks, adding marshmallows as needed to help form peaks. Spread icing between layers, sprinkling coconut on top of the icing as you stack the layers. Cover the outside of the whole cake with icing and sprinkle coconut on top of it.

Chocolate Cherries

Shortly after my father died, I came to visit with my mom. One day I saw her crying while she was looking at an empty box from some chocolate-covered cherries. She told me it was the last present my dad had given her. He had always given her a box of that candy every year. They were farmers and very poor—so poor sometimes that a little box of candy was the only present he could afford to get her. He always put a box of them under the tree for her.

I watched as she sat there holding that box and going through all the memories of Christmas in her mind. The next year I got a box of them and placed it under the tree with her name on it. When she unwrapped that gift, everyone in the family started crying. Every year since then there has been a box of chocolate-covered cherries under the tree with Mom's name on it. Our tradition at Christmas came from a gesture of love that grew quietly over the years.

— AARON WILBURN

My Son's Home

I was one of the first to go to Korea with the 1st Marine Division in 1950 and was, therefore, one of the first allowed to come home. It was just before Christmas 1951. The look on my mother's face as we ate Christmas dinner will always be with me. It was around Thanksgiving the year before that the Chinese entered the Korean War and I was near the Chosin Reservoir when it happened. To say all hell broke loose is an understatement. I know my mother was thanking the good Lord that I had made it and was home with her that Christmas. It was a moment I will never forget.

— LES BEASLEY

Cotton Patch Christmas

I grew up on a cotton farm in Mississippi; in fact, my mother is ninety years old and still lives in the very house where I was born. My earliest days were spent in the cotton patch where my imagination transformed the hoe handle into a microphone as I dreamed of the day I'd travel all over the world singing gospel music and leave all that hard work behind.

Although our days were filled with hard work, Christmas was one day we were allowed to play and we took full advantage of it. The highlight for me was what we called a 'cooked fruitcake.' That's pretty misleading, because it really wasn't a fruitcake at all, but oh, how I loved it! First, Mama would bake those layers that were a mile high, and then she'd slather on that rich, thick, brown-sugary icing—the kind that tastes like she pulled down one of the clouds from heaven, mixed it with a mother's love, then used it to frost that cake. The finishing touch was perhaps the most important. She'd cover the top with those sugarcoated candies, orange slices and the like, and then she'd press English walnuts all over the sides. I know she still wishes she felt like getting in her kitchen and making that cake today.

The thing I remember most about this cake is how pretty it was. Mama really made it festive for us!

— ANN DOWNING

RECIPE FOR ANN'S COOKED FRUITCAKE

1 stick butter

1/2 cup shortening

2 cups sugar

1 cup buttermilk

5 eggs, separated

2 cups self rising flour

1 cup blackberry jam

1 cup walnuts

1 teaspoon vanilla

Cream margarine and shortening, then add sugar and beat well until smooth. Add egg yolks and beat well. Alternately, add flour and buttermilk to cream mixture, and then stir in vanilla, nuts and jam. Fold in egg whites and pour into 3 greased and floured 8-inch cake pans. Bake at 325-degree oven for 25 minutes or until cake is done.

ICING

1/2 stick margarine (or butter)

2 cups sugar

1 teaspoon vanilla

1 cup chopped nuts

1/2 cup raisins

1/2 cup coconut

Beat margarine and sugar together; add vanilla, nuts, raisins, and coconut and beat until smooth. Spread between layers and on top of cake. Decorate with jellied orange slices, gumdrops, whole English walnuts and any candy you would like to add.

For Whom the Bells Toll

An old friend named Claudel asked me to sing at her husband's funeral. I was surprised when she said it was one of Carl's last requests that I sing "Jingle Bells" at his service. But I got up there and tried to fulfill my friend's wishes by singing "Jingle Bells" just as mournful as I could for the funeral. It got so embarrassing that the funeral directors walked out. Afterwards, Claudel thanked me, but she added, 'There was so much going on; I don't know what I was thinking. I really meant to ask you to sing, "When They Ring Them Golden Bells," not "Jingle Bells".'

—TONY GREENE

Midnight Fudge and Memories

When we get together with our big extended family on Christmas Eve, we make Midnight Fudge—it takes just three minutes to make. The child who has just learned to read that year gets to read the Christmas story aloud to us all. We then take turns telling one thing we are thankful for before we open presents. Reggie and I have dinner together and do the same, just the two of us, before we go and visit family. We go caroling to nursing homes and shut-ins. Even though we are sometimes exhausted from touring, when we start singing for people who need cheering up, it energizes us and we are the ones who get blessed.

I always remember my mother at Christmas because she loved to decorate. She was also an incredible cook, and she had certain traditional dishes she always fixed along with one recipe she'd never tried before. She made every event memorable.

—LADYE LOVE SMITH

I love all Christmas food and desserts except for...
FRUITCAKE!

—IVAN PARKER

Here's a recipe that even fruitcake haters love:

RECIPE FOR GLORIA'S MOIST & CHEWY CHRISTMAS FRUITCAKE

2-1/2 cups of sifted flour

1 teaspoon of baking soda

2 eggs

1 jar of None-Such mincemeat
   (with rum and brandy)

1 -15 oz. can condensed milk

1/2 cup of applesauce

1 cup of English walnut pieces

1 cup of red, candied cherries

1/2 cup of candied pineapple pieces

1/2 cup of green candied cherries

4 pineapple rings

Apricot Mixture:

3 cups of apricot nectar

1/2 cup white Karo Syrup

1/4 cup rum or brandy
   (or two teaspoons of rum flavoring)

DIRECTIONS:

Preheat oven to 300 degrees. Butter and flour two bread pans or four mini-bread pans (fruitcake size). Combine baking soda and flour. Combine eggs, mincemeat, condensed milk, fruit and nuts. Fold in dry ingredients. Divide evenly between the pans. Garnish the top with candied pineapple rings, a few cherries and walnut halves. Bake slowly at 300 degrees until the straw inserted in the center comes out clean. This should take about 40 minutes for small pans, 1 hour for larger pans. While the cake is baking, heat in a saucepan the 3 cups of apricot nectar, 1/2 cups of white Karo Syrup and 1/4 cup of rum or brandy (or 1 teaspoon of rum flavoring). When cake is done, poke fork holes in the top of each cake while still hot in the pans and soak the cakes with the hot apricot mixture until they can't absorb any more. Cool cakes, remove from pans, wrap in plastic wrap and then wrap in foil. Refrigerate at least a week before serving (if you can keep someone from sneaking a piece in the night).

Go tell it on the mountain,

Over the hills and everywhere.

Go tell it on the mountain,

That Jesus Christ is born!

A Christmas Play to Remember

Having a new baby every other Christmas for the past nine years has been our only consistent tradition to date! Just keeping up with all the energy in our house has made this an exciting time of our lives. With five boys, our Christmas memories are constantly evolving. My favorite memory to date is the Christmas when my wife, Angela, put together a children's Christmas play with the kids in our neighborhood. Around the end of September, she started what she called Kids' Club here at our farm on Saturdays. She had written a little play for the kids to perform that would pull together the stories of creation, mankind's fall from grace, and redemption, ending with the Christmas story.

The children met every week at our house for a time of playing games, learning their parts, and munching refreshments. By the time December twenty-third approached, they were very excited to perform for their friends and family. We set the play in our big old barn and decorated it with lights, the Garden of Eden, the hillside for the shepherds, and a rustic manger. Inside the barn we had Christmas cakes, cookies, and candies set up around a fire with a big black kettle of hot apple cider for all. I roped off a parking area half a mile from the barn and shuttled everyone into the play with my tractor and hay wagon. It was great fun. We hosted around 120 people and the children thoroughly enjoyed performing for everyone.

I wrapped up the event with an explanation of how we can know Jesus in a personal way. We finished up eating and drinking cider around a big fire. We had two inches of fresh snow on the ground, so you can imagine how picturesque it was. I was really proud of my wife and children.

—GUY PENROD

Daddy's Little Girl

My most wonderful Christmas memory was the year my daughter turned four years old. Four-year-old girls are just fabulous—they love all holidays. My little girl's favorite present was a 'my size' doll who wore the same size clothes she did. It was so cute to see her playing with that doll—I'll never forget her delight in the present and how she charmed everyone into joining in her fun.

But the gifts weren't the main reason she loved Christmas. She was never one to go overboard about the gifts. Even though children are bombarded with commercialism every year, my daughter has always had such a true heart about the real meaning of Christmas—from the time she was just a tiny girl to today when she has grown into a beautiful woman of God. She keeps me on track and helps me realize what Christmas is all about.

—WOODY WRIGHT

Stage Struck

When I was nine, I had a crush on my Sunday school teacher who was also the church pianist. One day she asked me to sing "The First Noel" for Christmas and I couldn't tell her no, even though the idea of singing in front of the whole church scared me to death. I was so shy I couldn't look at the audience at all as I sang. I just kept my eyes on her. I didn't finish the whole song. I sang the first verse and the chorus, and then I said, 'That's enough!' and sat down.

—JESSIE DIXON

Refrigerator Truck

It was the seventies and The Downings were enjoying their heyday. Paul and I had just bought our dream house and finished remodeling it. To celebrate, we threw a truly fancy dinner party at Christmas time. We set the table with silver and fine china and served countless courses. But behind the scenes, things were not as polished. You see, my mother-in-law had made more custard than could ever possibly fit in the refrigerator. Fortunately, it was freezing outside, and we were able to refrigerate our fancy dessert on the hood of Paul's old pickup truck parked just outside the kitchen door!

— ANN DOWNING

RECIPE FOR **OLD FASHIONED CHRISTMAS CUSTARD**

This is the custard recipe Paul's mother
made for all our gospel music friends:

1 quart milk
6 eggs
3/4 cup sugar

1 tablespoon cornstarch
2 teaspoons vanilla
1 small container whipped cream

DIRECTIONS:

Beat eggs. Mix cornstarch and sugar and add to eggs. Bring
milk to boiling point. Add egg mixture as you stir. Cook until
it coats the spoon and thickens. Pour and cool. Whip the cream
and add to cooled custard. Makes 1-1/2 quarts.

Shoebox Presents

"Away in a Manger" is my favorite Christmas song for the same reason "Jesus Loves Me" is one of my favorite songs. Those songs I learned as a child have grown with me. They are as real to sing as a fifty-year-old as they were when I was a five-year-old.

I try to ignore the commercial hoopla around Christmas. My wife and I surround ourselves with friends, baking, music, and activities that show the real reason for Christmas. For the last few years we have put together hundreds of shoeboxes of Christmas gifts for the orphans in Belarus who would not have presents any other way. Then as we open our gifts, we think about those kids opening their gifts. We always spend Christmas Eve talking about the birth of Christ and sit by the fireplace with the children. There's something about telling that story that makes it come to life as if Jesus were being born just down the street in a barn. Your heart just tells you 'This is not a fairy tale; this is the real thing.'

—AARON WILBURN

Christmas Homecoming

You can tell how much our family loves Christmas by the
name we gave our grandson. But another reason for his name was
that our family was hoping December twenty-fifth would become
a milestone day for us the year he was born. The reason for this hope
was that on October of 1993 our little grandson, Nicolas Christmas, was
born three months premature. Christmas was a special date that we had marked on
the calendar for reasons other than the holiday. We waited anxiously from October fifteenth until
December twenty-fifth for him to grow from two pounds up to five pounds. He grew steadily and
finally, he was allowed to come home on Christmas Day.

— LABREESKA HEMPHILL

Peace that Passes Understanding

After fifty years of living with Brock, I got used to doing holiday things with him. I'm so thankful for my family and friends because they have stood by me. I always have the hope and knowledge that God is with me. I have found out there is a peace in Him that I've never fully understood before.

—FAYE SPEER

Hope in Christ

My father left us a life we can pattern our lives by and that's a treasure. Even though we miss him terribly since he passed away, we know that there is still hope and remember songs like "Never Say Goodbye". We know he's in heaven and that gives us hope to keep going. If you've lost someone you love, I want you to know there is hope in Christ. He can give you deep joy in your heart even when you are going through grief and sorrow.

—KELLY NELON

Fire!

When I was a young girl, my family attended the Parksville Baptist Church where my mother was the custodian. She always cleaned the building on Saturdays and my little brother and I helped her. One Saturday, after working all morning, mother took us to the little general store next door for sandwiches. The owner of the store was surprised to see us because he had heard that the fire department had been called to our address.

Mother rushed us to our street where we saw our small home engulfed in flames. We could only watch as the firemen tried unsuccessfully to arrest the fire. My grandfather was very relieved to see us because he had believed we were sleeping upstairs. The firemen had wrestled him to the ground after he had attempted to enter the burning door to find us. We had lost everything just before Christmas time, but we were thankful that we were all safe.

One day shortly afterward, my best friends,

Nancy and Kim Edwards, stopped by to ask if I wanted to ride their pony. I went off with them, glad to be with my buddies. While we were out, the girls said they wanted to 'stop by' our church youth leaders' house. As soon as we arrived, all of my church friends came running out the back door yelling 'Surprise!' They had planned a party just for me. My wonderful friends gave me presents to replace all that I had lost. They gave me clothes, makeup, a record player with a whole box of 45's, shoes, hats—everything a girl could need.

Since then Christmas always reminds me of my friends' generosity and I look for opportunities to give to others as I remember God's gift of His Son.

—ALLISON DURHAM SPEER

The Good Times

I keep replaying the Christmas in the Country Homecoming video to see my favorite part. It shows my brother, Danny sitting there in the front row smiling, enjoying everything. He was feeling well—the best he had felt in a long time since his battle with cancer had begun. After that time, his health deteriorated and he was not able to go out of the house much. That video is bittersweet because it not only reminds me of the loss of my brother, but also of the loss of our good friend, Bob Cain. Bob doesn't actually appear on the video because he passed away before he could come to that Homecoming gathering. The joy we had in spite of our loss was great. Those two memories make that gathering especially important to me. As I get older, I hate to see good things come to an end. I find myself cherishing the blessing that we still have my mom and dad with us. I'm always thankful for my wife and kids, and Christmas magnifies that strong feeling I have for them throughout the year.

If I could share one message with people regarding what Christmas is all about, it would be found in the two great commandments of Christ: Love God with real passion and love each other from your heart. I think if we could do those two things; all the other things would fall into place. If I had a mission statement for what we are doing with our lives it would be 'loving God and loving each other.'

Danny Gaither

Thank You; Lord, for the gift of Yourself.
Thank You that because of that gift,
You have made us one.
Make us ambassadors that break down walls
that separate and divide people.
Make us lovers that build bridges and reach across chasms.
Thank You for giving us the sweet assurance
that whether we sing on this side or the other side,
it is the Song that started on the Judean hill
that rings in our hearts: Glory to God in the highest
and on Earth peace, goodwill, love for all.
Amen.

—GLORIA GAITHER

Celebrate Christmas with Bill & Gloria Gaither and their Homecoming Friends!

Christmas is a time for joy and celebration. If you enjoy this book, the two newest Gaither Christmas videos, CHRISTMAS ... A TIME FOR JOY and CHRISTMAS IN THE COUNTRY would be a wonderful addition to your Homecoming video collection. Filmed at the beautiful Alabama Theatre in Birmingham, these incredible video and audio projects feature Homecoming favorites singing songs like: *Joy, To The World; O Little Town of Bethlehem; Silent Night, Holy Night; Angels We Have Heard On High; White Christmas; Away In A Manger; I'll Be Home For Christmas* and many, many others.

Available wherever music is sold.

PICTURED FROM LEFT TO RIGHT: BILL AND GLORIA GAITHER, KELLY NELON, REX NELON, AND GUY PENROD